A FIRST LOOK BOOK

Lasers

David Jefferis

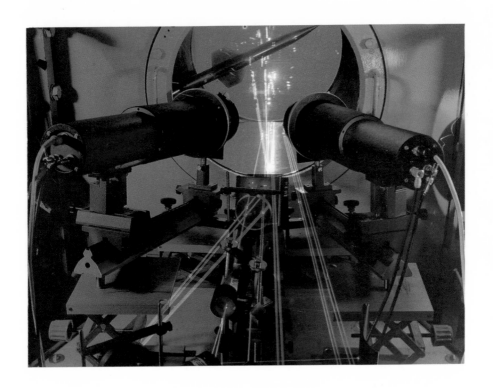

Franklin Watts

London   New York   Toronto   Sydney

© 1986 Franklin Watts Ltd

First published in Great Britain
    1986 by
Franklin Watts
12a Golden Square
London W1

First published in the USA by
Franklin Watts Inc.
387 Park Avenue South
New York N.Y.10016

UK ISBN: 0 86313 357 6
US ISBN: 0-531-10164-9
Library of Congress Catalog Card
    Number 85-51601

Illustrated by
Rob and Rhoda Burns
Drawing Attention
Eagle Artists
Michael Roffe

Photographs supplied by
ASEA
Culham Laboratories
Chrysler Corporation
Richard Bowler
Light Fantastic
US Dept of Energy

Picture Research by
Penny Warne

Technical consultant
Dr. Laurence Holden/Advanced
Holographics Ltd

Printed in Great Britain by
    Cambus Litho, East Kilbride

A FIRST LOOK BOOK

Lasers

Contents

What is a laser?

A laser is a machine which shines an intense beam of light. Lasers are used for many purposes. Lasers can illuminate a pop concert with coloured beams. Medium-power lasers enable surgeons to destroy cancers and other dangerous growths. High-power lasers can burn through steel and even destroy missiles in mid-air.

Laser light is different from ordinary light. The rays of a laser beam do not spread out as quickly as those of, for example, a torch. Laser light rays are usually the same colour. Ordinary "white" light is a mixture of the colours of the rainbow. Laser light rays are in step with each other – like marching troops, instead of a milling crowd.

A laser beam has light rays which are tightly packed, the same colour and moving in step. This makes a laser pack more energy, size for size, than any other light source.

△ A prism is a triangular glass block. It splits light into a spectrum, the colours of the rainbow, which mix to make white light.

Shine a laser through a prism and the beam stays the same colour – all the rays are the same shade.

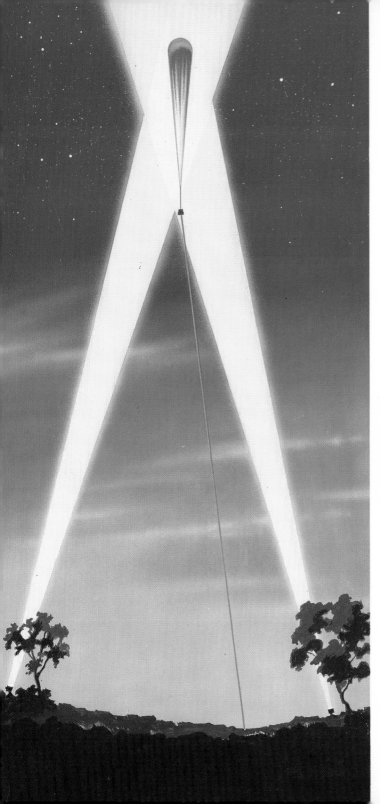

◁ Ordinary light spreads out, no matter how sharp the focus. Here, two searchlights shine on a weather balloon – you can see the fan-shaped spread of light. The laser remains a pencil-thin beam.

▽ These two screens show laser light (top), compared with the jumbled up patterns of ordinary light waves.

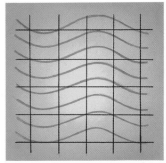

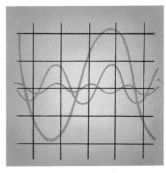

How a laser works

△ The picture above shows a typical laser.

Lasers vary in size from tiny ones, smaller than your finger, to monsters as big as a tower block. Large or small, they work in similar ways.

Energy is needed by any laser. Electrical discharge or powerful flash tubes are often used.

The energy is turned to laser light by the "active medium". This may be a

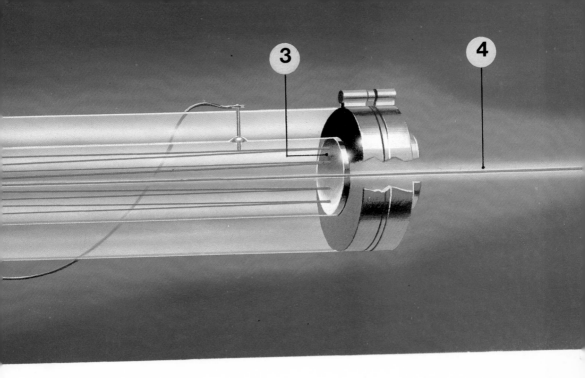

gas like carbon dioxide, or a liquid coloured with a dye. It may be a piece of crystal such as ruby. The type and colour of the laser beam changes according to the active medium used.

Laser energy bounces back and forth between two mirrors, one partially reflecting. In a tiny fraction of a second, the laser energy has built up into a torrent of power and bursts through the partially reflecting mirror. The energy shines through as a laser beam.

Laser beams are used in many roles, but all work like this.

1 Energy is pumped into the laser, usually as an electrical discharge or by using a flash tube.
2 Active medium changes energy to laser light.
3 Mirror system bounces light energy back and forth.
4 Laser beam.

The laser spectrum

We can see only a small part of the "electromagnetic spectrum". This is the whole range of wave energy found in nature, from radio and TV signals to X–rays and gamma rays. The part we see as light is a small bit in the middle.

A laser beam works in different parts of the spectrum according to the active medium used. Argon gas and ruby crystal shine as green and red beams. As the picture shows, many lasers have beams which lie outside our range of vision, and so are invisible.

▷ Here you see the range of energy found in nature. The part we can see is the visible-light spectrum. We can sense infra-red as heat, and ultra-violet can give us sunburn.

The other lasers marked have beams elsewhere in the spectrum. YAG stands for yttrium-aluminium-garnet – it is a man-made diamond, used as an active medium.

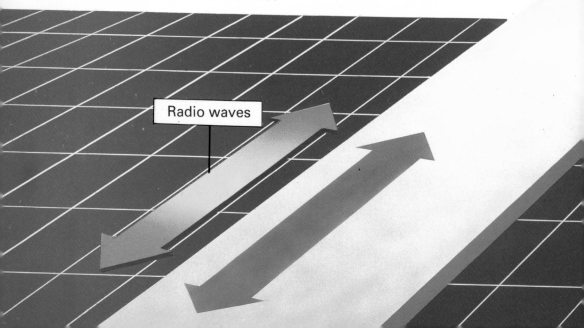

Radio waves

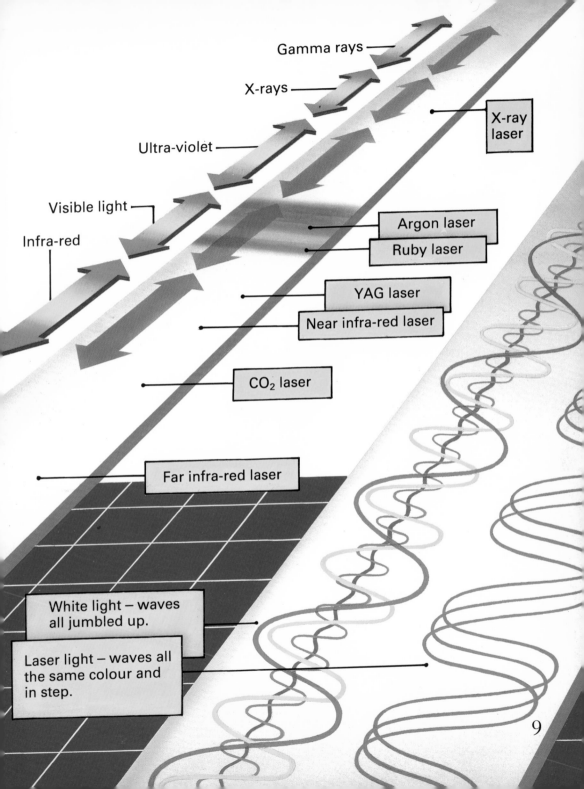

Gamma rays

X-rays

Ultra-violet

Visible light

Infra-red

X-ray laser

Argon laser

Ruby laser

YAG laser

Near infra-red laser

CO_2 laser

Far infra-red laser

White light – waves all jumbled up.

Laser light – waves all the same colour and in step.

9

Punching through steel

The laser is quite a new invention. The first one was tested in 1960 when American scientist Dr. Theodore Maiman switched on the world's first laser. Its active medium was a crystal of ruby.

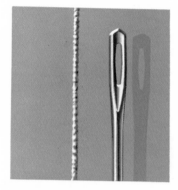

△ This picture shows a small needle compared to the join-line of two steel plates, welded together by laser beam.

The crystal produced a brief burst of bright red light. It was a pulsed laser, a type which releases its light in one flash. It then stores up more energy, releasing it in turn as another flash of light.

Light from pulsed lasers can be emitted in millionths of a second. For this short period of time, a tremendous amount of power can be focused on a target. Short pulses can cut through thick sheets of steel or even make materials explode.

Other lasers produce a constant beam. These are known as Continuous Wave, or CW lasers. They are not as powerful as pulsed lasers.

◁ A high-power laser pulses ten times a second to punch its way through hard steel.

▽ Below left, a factory robot uses a CW laser to clean off surface dirt from metal materials. The laser is just powerful enough to vaporize the dirt without damaging the raw material underneath.

The man on the right is preparing the next piece of material, ready for cleaning.

Talking with light

△ This laser telephone needs a clear line-of-sight between the two people wanting to talk. Once lined-up in the viewfinder, you can talk just by pressing a button.
1 Viewing system.
2 Laser receiver.
3 Laser transmitter.
4 Headphones.

The laser is a good alternative to TV and radio for long-distance communication. Much more information can be packed into a light beam than a radio signal or telephone cable.

Laser telephones like the one above are suitable for special purposes. The one shown is a military model which uses an invisible infra-red beam. But equipment like this needs a clear view as trees, buildings, fog or thick cloud

12

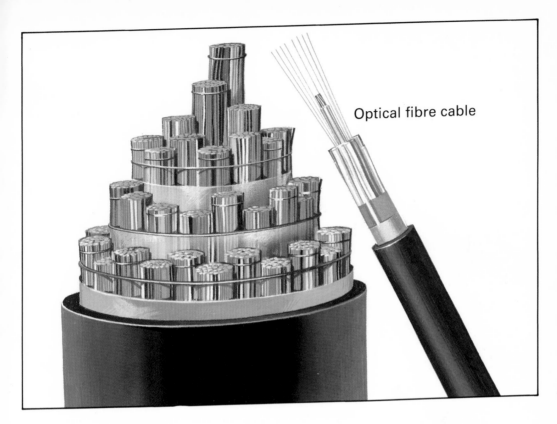

Optical fibre cable

break the signal.

The biggest future for laser communications is with optical fibres. These are very fine glass strands which guide light along their lengths. With booster repeaters every few kilometres, a laser message can be sent along an optical fibre for very long distances.

Optical fibres can be laid underground in much the same way as present-day telephone cables.

△ The big multistranded cable is a telephone cable. This one can carry 6,000 conversations, requiring 12,000 wires. The eight fibres of the optical fibre cable can carry 7,680 conversations.

The latest optical fibre cables, containing about 144 strands (only about as thick as your finger), can carry about 50,000 simultaneous conversations.

13

Lasers in supermarkets

△ The bar code is now found on many goods in supermarkets. See if you can spot the bar codes on these foods from seven countries.

Look out for bar codes on goods in your own home.

Lasers are used in many supermarkets to speed up queues at the check-out counters.

The Universal Product Code, or UPC, is the secret of fast check-outs. "Bar Codes" are printed on packages and all the assistant has to do is pass the striped pattern over a glass window by the till.

A low-power laser shines on the bar code pattern. Some light, or "back-

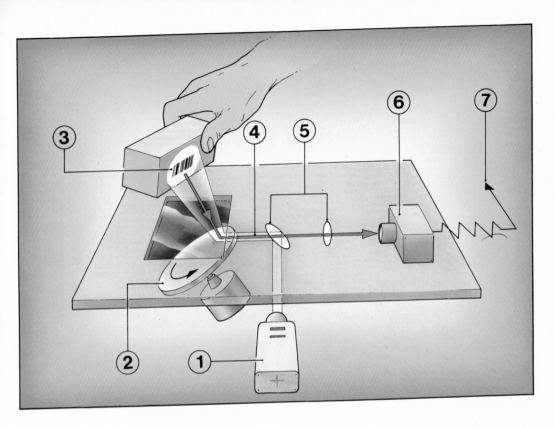

scatter", is reflected back. A detector converts the laser reflection to electronic pulses which are flashed to the store computer.

The computer compares the bar code pattern with those in its memory, which takes a fraction of a second, and signals the check-out cash till with the price. The computer can also print a receipt and keep the store's stock-list up to date.

△ This diagram shows how a bar code system works.
1 Low-power laser sends out a beam, reflecting off a mirror.
2 Beam passes through scanning disc and glass window.
3 Beam shines on bar code.
4 Backscatter reflected back.
5 Mirror and lens.
6 Detector.
7 Signal to store computer.

Discs and lightshows

△ Lasers are much used in the pop and disco world. Here a rock group performs to the light of multiple laser beams.

Lasers are used for information and for entertainment. Laser light has developed into an art form with rock shows, disco lights and son-et-lumiére displays.

Compact discs are gradually replacing LP records. Sound information is imbedded in microscopic pits under the lower surface of the disc. A laser reads off the information as the disc spins in the player. A great advan-

tage of the system is that there is no way a needle can scratch in the grooves.

Videodiscs are larger and can play back pictures as well as sound. The information is also buried in data pits and read by laser. The data pits are so tiny – hundreds could fit on a pinhead – that each side of a videodisc can store the text of thousands of books or up to 54,000 colour TV pictures.

△ This experimental in-car videodisc system contains an atlas and other map information. A computer in the car uses a satellite in space to get a navigational "fix". It then displays the car's position on a small TV screen. As the vehicle moves, the computer changes the TV map, updating the picture from the videodisc information store.

Surveying jobs

△ Lasers enable scientists to measure the Moon's distance from Earth with high precision.

Laser beams travel in straight lines, which makes them perfect for jobs where accuracy is needed. Lasers are used to align tunnels, check whether buildings are straight, and even to guide saws in logging mills.

Pulsed lasers are ideal for timing and distance measurements. By timing the return of reflected laser energy, very precise measurements can be taken.

The distance between Earth and Moon has been measured using special mirrors left on the Moon by American astronauts and Russian robot probes. Using a high-power pulsed ruby laser, scientists have measured the distance to an accuracy of a few centimetres.

LIDAR stands for Light-wave Detection And Ranging. It works by bouncing laser light off distant targets and measuring the returns. LIDAR can detect tiny particles, such as dirty specks in polluted air.

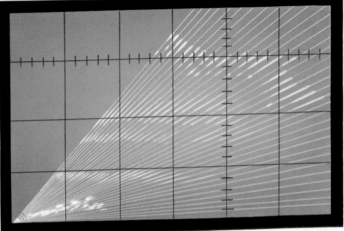

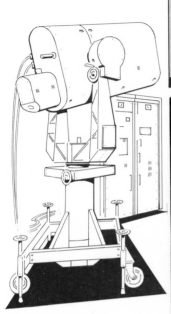

△ LIDAR is used to check atmospheric pollution, for example. Above, the mobile equipment. Top right, a diagram showing the beam reflecting off cloud and factory smoke. At right is the LIDAR display; it looks like a radar screen.

▷ Lasers are used to check straight-and-level in many building operations. Here a laser checks if a tunnel is straight.

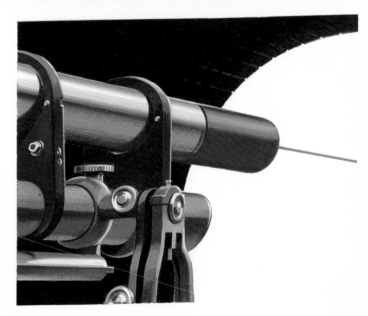

19

Life savers

▽ The endoscope can be used in throat and stomach operations. Features of the hand-held instrument are:
1 Laser.
2 Forceps.
3 Suction tube to remove waste fluid and gas.
4 Viewing lens.

The laser has become an important surgical tool.

The endoscope, shown below, is used to avoid cutting the body open in stomach operations for example. The flexible tube of the endoscope is passed down the throat. Once in the stomach, the end can be twisted and turned to let the surgeon inspect the problem.

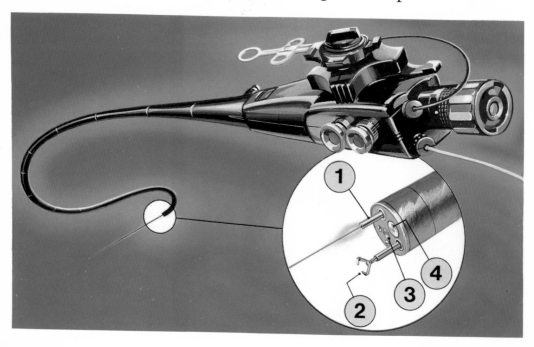

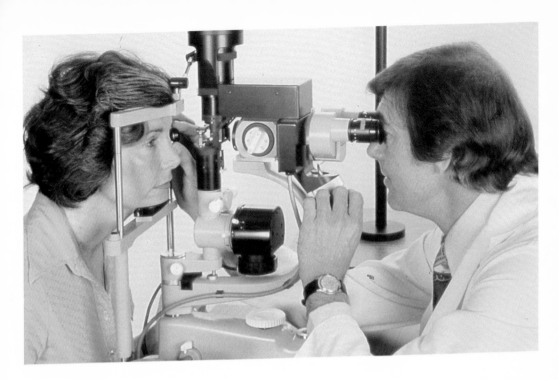

Light is provided by optical fibre and vision by a tiny viewing lens. The surgeon looks through a microscope-like eyepiece. Forceps can then be used to extract bits of tissue.

The surgeon can use a laser beam to destroy a dangerous growth in the stomach wall. The laser is a separate unit in the operating theatre. Its light is guided down the endoscope by optical fibre. Other major laser uses are for eye surgery. Blood vessels can be sealed and growths destroyed.

△ A laser is used here to check a patient's eyesight. Surgical lasers are used for many eye operations including tumour removal. Tumours are unwanted growths in the body. Some do no harm, while others are highly dangerous.

Holography

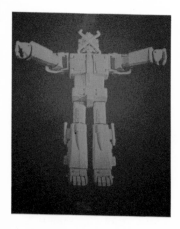

△ This hologram, of a robot from a Japanese TV series, is typical of the ghostly appearance of such a picture. You really feel like you can reach out and touch the object.

Holography involves the use of lasers to make three-dimensional pictures.

Viewing a hologram is like looking through a window. Floating mysteriously in the glass is a ghostlike image. By moving from side to side, you can look around, above or below the object to see it in three dimensions.

Holograms can be printed, but at the moment, truly accurate full-colour holograms are rare, experimental and expensive.

What use is a 3-D picture? There are many possibilities, including X-ray holography. This idea, when perfected, will enable scientists to probe deep into the microscopic world. Three-dimensional pictures of cells may become a tool for medical advance. A holographic data store could provide computer memory enough to fit a vast amount of information into a space smaller than a sugar cube.

△ Holograms are almost impossible to copy. Many credit card companies have introduced them to prevent forgeries. Here you can see holograms of a dove, the letters MC and three circles.

▷ This view looks through an aircraft windshield. A hologram reflects vital information, such as speed and height, from a TV tube into the pilot's eyes.

Smart weapons

▽ This battlefield shows lasers in combat action.
1 Plane points with a laser beam at a target.
2 Tank reflects some laser energy, called backscatter (dotted lines).
3 Smart shell homes in on the backscatter.
4 Laser beam from helicopter hits tank.

"Smart" is the military name for weapons which are guided very accurately to their targets by computer. Many of them use lasers.

A typical smart weapon uses a plane to point a laser at a target, such as an enemy tank. A smart shell is fired towards the target, from a gun or a friendly tank. A sensor in the shellhead

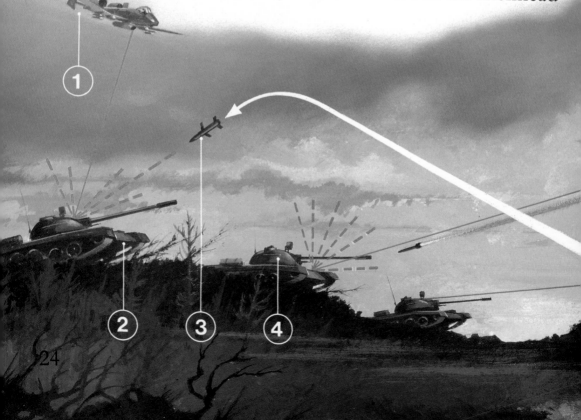

spots the laser light bounced off the target. A mini-computer in the shell moves small steering fins to guide the shell dead-on target.

Future uses for battlefield lasers include high-power types now being tested. Such lasers could blind tanks by destroying their viewports. Lasers have even destroyed missiles in mid-flight.

But for every advance, defences are often developed. These could include tiny, hard-to-hit windows and special laser armour.

5 Helicopter fires a missile which can detect backscatter.
6 Helicopters like this AH-64 can carry up to 16 missiles.
7 Tank fires smart shells.
8 Future artillerymen fire a high-power laser. This can blind tank gunsights. It can even punch through thin armour and destroy missiles in flight.

Lasers in space

◁ This scene could become reality in the future. A laser armed hunter-killer spacecraft fires a laser blast to destroy an enemy satellite. Opponents of such schemes argue that the cost is likely to be huge. Also, hunter-killers or space stations could be fooled by decoys and other countermeasures.

Experimental lasers have already been into Earth orbit aboard spacecraft. In the near future, laser beams will be useful for communications. There is no air to disturb a laser beam as it tracks across space.

Research shows that high-power military lasers could be aboard spacecraft in the 1990s. Military uses for such lasers are many.

Spacecraft, armed with lasers, could fly in orbit ready to strike at an enemy satellite. A powerful beam could melt radio aerials or even punch through a satellite's skin and wreck the delicate instruments inside.

Orbiting space stations could spot enemy missiles taking off from their bases on Earth. As the missiles climb out of the atmosphere, so the laser-armed space stations could pick them off and destroy them before they reach their targets.

Hot as the Sun

A more peaceful line of research is that of laser fusion. Early in the 21st century, fusion generators may provide electricity more cheaply and with less pollution than present-day power plants.

In the laboratory, laser fusion works like this: a ring of lasers fire at a tiny pellet of hydrogen fuel. Under the burst of high power laser energy, the pellet's shell explodes inwards, crushing the atoms at the pellet's core. As the atoms are forced together, they release energy. The result is a controlled atomic explosion.

In a power station, the heat would be used to boil water. The superheated steam would then spin turbines to generate electricity.

But work on laser fusion is still experimental. Much research remains to be done before such a power station can be built.

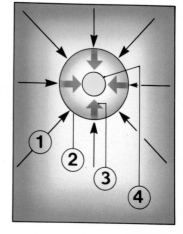

△ This diagram shows the principle of laser fusion.
1 Laser beams.
2 Fuel pellet.
3 Lasers destroy shell, forcing energy inwards.
4 Atoms at core crushed together. This process, called fusion, gives off energy.

▷ The picture shows an experimental laser fusion system. In the future, equipment like this may provide safe power from the atom.

28

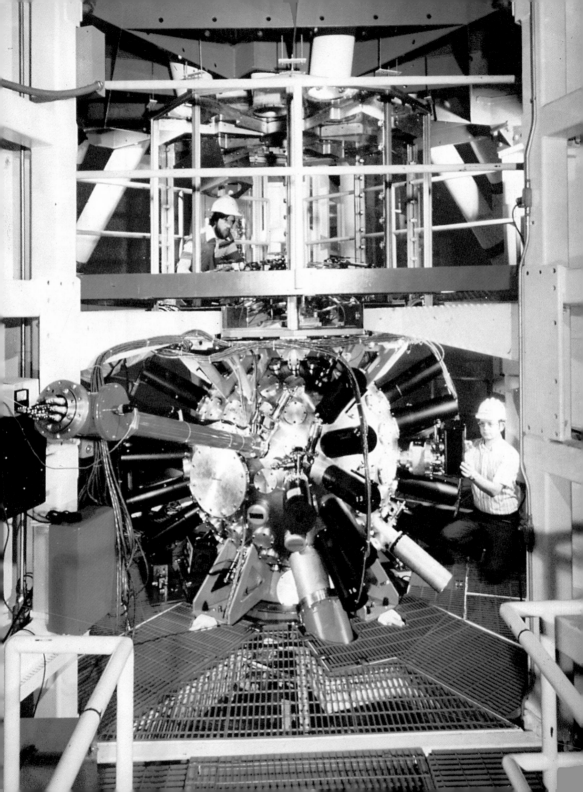

Future possibilities

Here are some areas in which lasers may be used in the future.

Laser computer
Present-day computers are limited by the speed at which electronic signals can move along the wires.

Using lasers and optical fibres, the speed of operation could be multiplied many times. Laser light is far quicker than an electronic pulse.

Talking to submarines
Subs can be out of touch with base for weeks at a time. By surfacing, a sub reveals its position to an enemy.

Blue-green lasers can penetrate ocean depths. Using the laser aboard a satellite, a commander could issue orders to a submarine at any time.

Laser starship
This is a sailing ship of space, propelled by the tiny, but constant push of light pressure.
1 Sun.
2 High-power laser, powered by solar cells.
3 Laser beam.
4 Starship. Made of tissue-thin metal foil, it is 1,000 km (621 miles) across. A small payload module is carried in the middle.
5 Direction of travel.

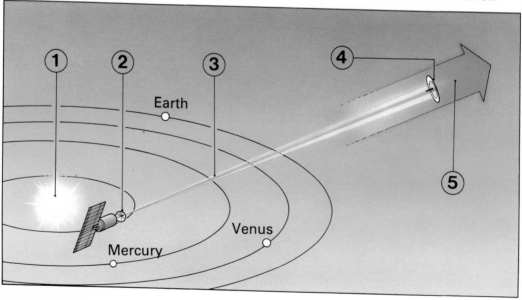

Earth

Mercury

Venus

Glossary

Here is a list of some of the technical words in this book.

Active medium
Part of a laser that generates laser light when energy is pumped in. Can be a gas, coloured liquid or a crystal.

Argon laser
Green laser that uses argon gas as its active medium.

Backscatter
Reflected laser energy.

Bar Code
Name for the UPC or Universal Product Code.

Coherent
Quality of laser light: the light waves move in step, like marching soldiers.

CW laser
Continuous wave laser. One that emits a beam as long as it is switched on. A pulsed laser emits a beam in short flashes.

Electromagnetic Spectrum
The entire range of wave energy found in nature. Radio waves and gamma rays are at two extremes. Visible light is a tiny part in the middle.

Feedback mechanism
The mirror assembly which bounces laser light back and forth until it has enough energy to emerge as a laser beam.

Head-up display
System used on aircraft for projecting flight information on aircraft windscreen.

Holography
Making 3-D pictures using lasers.

Infra-red
Part of the electro-magnetic spectrum we feel as heat. Infra-red lasers are invisible.

Laser
The word is short for Light Amplification by Stimulated Emission of Radiation.

Optical fibre
Glass fibre strand along which light can pass.

Prism
Triangular glass block. Splits light up into its various colours.

Ruby laser
Red coloured laser that uses a crystal of ruby as its active medium. Many other crystals can be used. YAG, for example, is a piece of synthetic crystal.

Ultra-violet
Beyond the violet end of the visible spectrum. We cannot see it, but can sometimes feel the results of too much exposure, when we suffer from sunburn.

31

Index